Affiliate Cash

How To Make Money As An Affiliate Marketer

By

Omar Johnson

© 2013 Omar Johnson and Make Profits Easy LLC

Table of Contents

1. What is Affiliate Marketing and How Does It Work? 7
   - What is Affiliate Marketing Used For? 8
   - Does This Type of Marketing Really Work? 9
   - Why You Would Start Affiliate Marketing 10
   - How Does Affiliate Marketing Really Work? 10
   - How Much Commission Can You Make? 11
   - Could There Be Any More Positives? 12
2. Making Money with Affiliate Marketing – It Can Be Done! 14
   - Choose Carefully 15
   - Track and Analyze 16
   - Tracking Devices 16
   - Aligning the Product or Service with the Audience 17
   - Reviews 17
   - Be Part of a Team 18
   - A Sales Page 18
   - You *Can* Be A Successful Affiliate Marketer! 18
   - Choose a Few Great Products 19
   - Use More than One Traffic Source 19
   - Know if There Is a Demand 19
   - Keep Current 20
   - Choosing a Merchant 20

- Use the Tools .... **Error! Bookmark not defined.**
3. The Main Marketing Tools 21
    1. Blogging for Affiliate Marketing 21
        Setting Up an Affiliate Blog 22
    2. Affiliate Landing Page 24
    3. Affiliate Marketing Website 25
        Different Types of Affiliate Marketing Websites 26
    4. Killer Content Necessary! 26
        - Videos 27
        - Email Subject Lines 27
        - Pre-sells and Sales Letters 27
        - Headlines 28
        a. Blogging 29
        b. Video 29
        c. Social Media 29
    5. Google Analytics 30
        1. Tracking Email Signups 30
        2. Tracking Clicks on Affiliate Links 30
        3. Tracking Clicks on Google Adsense Ads 31
        4. Tracking Clicks on Other Adverts 31
    6. PayPal 33
4. Getting the Leads 34
    Online Lead Generation 34

- Facebook Marketing 35
  - A Few Facebook Marketing Tips 37
- Solo Ads.. 38
- Pay-Per-Click Marketing... 39
5. How to Find an Affiliate Program That's Right for You 41
  - 1. The Product or Service 41
  - 2. Website 42
  - 3. Conversion Rate 43
  - 4. Commission or Payout 43
  - 5. Average Order Value 44
  - 6. Earnings Per Click (EPC)... 44
  - 7. Duration of Cookies... 45
  - 8. Tools 46
  - 9. Reversal Rates 46
  - 10. Competition 47
  - 11. Terms of Service.. 47
  - 12. Support... 48
6. Popular Affiliate Programs 49
  - 1. Clickbank 49
  - 2. Linkshare 50
  - 3. Amazon Associates.. 50
  - 4. Commission Junction 51
  - 5. RevenueWire.. 51

- 6. Ebay Partner Network 52
- 7. ShareASale 52
- 8. OneNetworkDirect 52
- 9. AvantLink 52
- 10. Google Affiliate Network 52

7. Mistakes New Affiliate Marketers Should Avoid 54
- 1. Thinking You're Going to Get Rich Quickly 54
- 2. Assuming People Will Just Visit Your Site 54
- 3. Bombarding Your Audience 54
- 4. On the Other Hand: Not Providing Enough Material . 55
- 5. Not Measuring Performance 55
- 6. Neglecting To Gauge Your Competition 55
- 7. Not Choosing Your Affiliate Partners Carefully 56
- 8. Not Providing Your Audience with Quality Content .. 56
- 9. Not Understanding What You're Promoting 56
- 10. Overselling to Your Market 57
- 11. Making False Claims 57

Becoming an Affiliate Marketer 58

1. What is Affiliate Marketing and How Does It Work?

According to *entrepreneur.com*, affiliate marketing is defined as:

A way for a company to sell its products by signing up individuals or companies ("affiliates") who market the company's products for commission.

There are two ways in which you can approach this type of marketing. You can either offer an affiliate program to other people or you can sign up to be an affiliate yourself. If you are the business driving the program, you will pay your affiliates a commission for every single lead or sale that they drive to your website. The goal here is to find affiliates who can reach untapped markets.

Affiliate marketing has undoubtedly become one of the most popular ways to make money online. The growth in popularity is due to the fact that this type of money maker is virtually free to set up and in fact, almost anyone can start doing it – no matter what age or background you come from.

Simply put, affiliate marketing is the process of selling someone else's products or services and receiving a commission in return for doing so. This is an attractive proposition if you have a website but perhaps no services or products of your own to market.

What is Affiliate Marketing Used For?

Basically, this type of marketing is used to grasp a wider target market than a company normally would reach. It is also used to increase customer bases and, most importantly, sales. It is a highly effective way to get a large number of people to promote, endorse and sell products or services in return for a commission.

Here's an example:

If you have your own business selling organic cleaning products it can be expensive and time consuming as the owner of the business to market the products alone. But, if you recruit, let's say 100 people (aka affiliates) to sell your products you could very quickly reach a much larger area, increase your customer base exponentially and therefore increase your sales. It also means you would only need to pay out money for marketing when products are sold via an affiliate's recommendation. This results in a highly viable marketing strategy for your company. Also, if those

100 affiliates that help to promote and sell your cleaning products receive a commission in return for every sale, they have strong incentive to continue promoting your products. So it's a win-win situation!

Does This Type of Marketing Really Work?

The simple answer is a resounding YES! There are many people who have been making regular incomes online as affiliates for many years. However, if you've read those advertisements about how affiliate marketing can easily make you thousands of dollars every day without doing much work, take heed! Work does need to be done to make that sort of cash.

Sure, you can make massive amounts of dough from this type of marketing and yes, there are people who do so every day, but they certainly didn't start off that way. In reality, it took them a good amount of time and effort to set up their affiliate marketing empires and only after a good amount of hard work are they reaping the rewards for their efforts.

Keep in mind from the very beginning that affiliate marketing is a business and a fantastic way to make money online, but it requires growth, time and effort in order to enjoy success. The great thing about this type of marketing, though, is that you can begin building a business almost immediately, for free!

Why You Would Start Affiliate Marketing

Besides being the perfect way to earn money, affiliate marketing includes a number of other pros:

- You don't have to purchase or rent business premises
- You don't have to deal with sales or customers directly
- You don't need to purchase or store inventory
- You don't have to deal with the packing and shipping of goods or deal with refunds
- You can run your business from anywhere in the world and start earning money 24/7 and best of all…
- You do not need huge amounts of capital to start your business

How Does Affiliate Marketing Really Work?

If the term "affiliate marketing" is starting to sound like an attractive prospect, but still a little confusing, let's break it down into how it really works.

The first step to making money via affiliate marketing starts with the customer. Ultimately, it is the customer who is going to make a purchase from the end seller and they are therefore the reason that you get paid a commission. The idea here is that you, as the affiliate, get the customer to visit your marketing platform such as your landing page, website, and social networks - pretty much anywhere you can place a link to drive the leads.

The prospect then clicks on the affiliate link. This link is typically given to you by the merchant that you are an affiliate of and your affiliate link can track all of your sales numbers and click-throughs. If the prospect decides to make a purchase from the website after arriving there via your link, you make the commission.

How Much Commission Can You Make?

Commission can vary greatly with affiliate marketing. Some companies are willing to pay a great deal of money for driving traffic to their websites. For example, some of the better known companies will pay as much as 10%. So if you end up sending a prospect to a 10% commission site via your affiliate link and they make a purchase of $200, for example, you will earn $20 off that sale.

There are some programs that will even pay as much as 75% commission on a sale. So if a product is $50 and you send a customer to the website to make that $50 purchase, you make as much as $37 – just for sending someone to a site that interests them!

Affiliate programs literally pay out billions of dollars every year. They allow people to successfully work from home, running their own business on their own time. A couple more incentives include:

- Setting your own schedule
- Running your business from anywhere as long as you have an internet connection
- Enjoying direct deposits from most companies so that your checks go straight into your bank account
- You can enjoy the things you've always wanted in life with your new income
- You are your own boss!

Could There Be Any More Positives?

There sure are! Just look at this list:

- You don't have to sell a thing. You just send people to the company's website and the seller takes care of everything else
- You don't need a big budget
- You don't have to be too technically-minded

- You do not have to provide customer support. The seller will take care of this

If you're starting to see how powerful affiliate marketing can be and want to learn more, read on to learn how money can be made through various channels and how to set those channels up.

In this book we will also cover how to get those all-important leads and of course, how to find an affiliate program that's right for you. We will also take a look at the most popular programs that are out there and some of the mistakes that you, as a new affiliate marketer, can avoid.

2. Making Money with Affiliate Marketing – It Can Be Done!

Affiliate marketing works by choosing the service or product you want to sell and the seller then provides you with a unique affiliate code which you then use to refer traffic to the seller's site.

Most programs offer ready-made banners, links or other forms of content and you simply have to copy a code and place it on your marketing platforms in order to begin referring traffic. When prospects click on the link they are redirected to the seller's site to make the purchase.

However, affiliate marketing is not only about selling a product or service to make a commission. In fact, different programs make use of different payment terms, for example:

- **Pay per lead** – you will be paid your commission once the referred visitors provide their contact information on the seller's website, usually by filling out a short contact form.
- **Pay per sale** – the most common form of affiliate marketing whereby the seller pays you a commission of the sale price once the purchase is complete.

- **Pay per click** – you will be paid based on the amount of visitors you redirect to the seller's website, regardless of whether a sale is made or not.

So there are actually numerous ways to successfully make money with affiliate marketing. Anyone who takes the time to learn the ropes and can apply what they learn can make good money online.

Successful affiliate marketers realize that it is important to make use of affiliate networks which are extremely useful in connecting webmasters to adverts of high interest. Also, working through networks will help you to build your reputation.

One of the most important points to remember if you want to be a prosperous affiliate marketer is to not become complacent. Continue seeking ways to increase profitability (as discussed in chapter 3).

If you're ready to get started as an affiliate marketer, below are some tips for doing it right.

- Choose Carefully

Try not to make a quick decision and jump on some sort of bandwagon product when you're starting out. Choose a product or service that genuinely interests you. If you're passionate about the product or service you will be better able to convince prospects to make that purchase. You'll also desire to learn more about the product or service and you'll be able to better place yourself as an authority that can provide engaging content. Knowledge of the service or product will quickly place you as an expert who is sincere and experienced.

- Track and Analyze

Once you have set up your affiliate marketing platforms and are populating them with fresh, convincing and knowledgeable content, you will need to analyze and track your platform's performance. Continuous analysis of performance will help you to continue improving your platforms as well as ensuring they are properly optimized (that is, they are popular amongst search engine rankings).

You can make use of affiliate system reporting to track clicks; impressions and even registrations so that you can determine precisely how your traffic interacts with your content.

- Tracking Devices

Having a super-hot website or blog is crucial but you also need to keep track of current devices. For example, last year alone, smartphone subscribers grew by almost 20% world-wide. Advertisements viewed on tablets increased by nearly 15% towards the latter half of 2012. So it's important to do your research and ensure that your platforms are "friendly" for various devices including tablets; PCs and mobile phones. Tracking how potential customers are interacting with the product you're promoting will help you to understand better where your focus ought to be.

- Aligning the Product or Service with the Audience

Aligning your product with your audience should go without saying. If you're promoting a product for female hormones, for example, you're not going to be sharing links to a male balding site or a link to a site about e-book writing.

- Reviews

Often affiliate marketers stick a banner up on their site or blog and leave it at that. They're left wondering why no one is purchasing their affiliate product or service. Think about this: when you're searching for a product, do you not search for reviews? Do you not want to know that other people think the product is great so that chances are you'll think so too?

Reviews are essential marketing tools that will help you to reel in prospects. Create compelling write-ups about your affiliate products or services so that you can entice customers to make that purchase. Once you've written the review, add customer testimonials and a couple of images or videos this will position you as an expert and authority that people will want to purchase from. This is one of the easiest and most effective ways to make money with online affiliate marketing.

- **Be Part of a Team**

Don't underestimate the power of a team to promote an affiliate product or service and help you to rake in the cash. Find a couple of influencers and contribute to their blogs or have them contribute to yours and together you can produce killer content to promote the product.

- **A Sales Page**

If you have a sales page that looks unprofessional, chances are buyers will think the same of the product or service you're promoting. If you want your product or service to be seen as top-notch, make sure your sales page is of high-quality.

You *Can* Be A Successful Affiliate Marketer!

We've already mentioned that you won't get rich over night with affiliate marketing but it is definitely an effective way to make money online. It is also extremely competitive. If you want to achieve financial freedom via this type of marketing, you need to know your market – what their needs are – in order to promote your affiliate product or service.

You will need to learn what will work and what won't. Below are a couple of tricks that will help you:

- **Choose a Few Great Products**

Often affiliates sign up to a whole lot of different programs and go about promoting everything they can. This can become overwhelming and you really won't be able to properly promote all the products you signed up for. Instead, choose a few great products and focus on those. Understand the target market's needs and align them with the appropriate products or services.

- **Use More than One Traffic Source**

You may want to put up advertisements on your site only. That's fine. But there are numerous traffic sources to be tapped into that can help you to promote the products. When it comes to affiliate marketing the bottom line is, the more traffic you can direct to the sales page, the better your chances are of making a substantial income as an affiliate marketer.

- **Know if There Is a Demand**

If you attempt to promote a product that has a low demand, chances are pretty good you're not going to get too many sales. So spend time researching the product and finding out if it is something your target audience needs.

- **Keep Current**

Stay current with new marketing techniques that are always coming up. Know the latest market trends and avoid falling behind.

- **Choosing a Merchant**

Promoting a product means you're also promoting the person (or company) behind that product. So it's a good idea to choose carefully. You don't want to encourage customers to buy a product they're not going to be happy with. You will lose visitors and credibility. Try to seek out companies or merchants that offer a good customer service and experience.

- **Use the Tools**

In the next chapter we discuss some of the main affiliate marketing tools. Find those that will help you to be efficient. Make sure that whichever tools you use that they are correctly set up. Don't just sit back and wait for visitors to click on your links and make purchases. Stay structured, follow a plan and then reap the rewards of affiliate marketing.

3. The Main Marketing Tools

When it comes to affiliate marketing you may not need a lot of capital to get started, but you will need knowledge and tools. You need to know what you're going to be promoting and who your target market is. Next, you're going to need the tools that will help you to entice leads; tell them about the product or service; share information and testimonials with them and, of course, you will need tools that will help you to monitor your platform's performance so that you can continue to successfully market the product or service to your visitors. You will also need an account so that you can receive payment of the commission you have earned as an affiliate marketer.

In this chapter we share a few of the necessary tools to get you started as an affiliate marketer.

1. Blogging for Affiliate Marketing

A blog is arguably one of the most essential marketing tools you could have and with the numerous free blogging platforms available, such as WordPress and Blogger.com, setting up a free blog is easy.

However, your blog is not only going to be about content. You need to ensure that it is technically set up with a good base and is optimized for sales. It also needs to be set up in a way that will help you build a list for future promotions. You can either choose to hire someone to set up your blog or you can choose to do it yourself, which is the perfect option if you don't have much of a start-up budget.

Setting Up an Affiliate Blog

1. Firstly, you'll need to register your domain (what you plan on calling your blog). Again, there are a variety of sites where you can do this, the most popular being GoDaddy. But you can purchase your domain from wherever you wish. A good tip is to go to Google and type in something along the lines of "GoDaddy coupon code for April 2013" or whichever year and month it is. This search will bring up a variety of results with codes and specials that will help you to save a heap of cash!
2. Next, you need hosting. Again, a simple Google search will help you to find the right host for your blog. Once you register you will receive your Nameservers. Write them down as you'll need them in the next step.
3. Next you can log into your domain registrar and point the nameservers to your newly set

up hosting account nameservers. Remember to save your changes.
4. You can then log into your chosen host and install your blog. The host page should be able to guide you through the process seamlessly. Make sure you give your blog the proper details such as admin name; password and site title. Save your additions.
5. When you first login to your new blog, you will need to set it up and choose your preferences for things like fonts, images and themes. Remember to add an About Page and you're ready for your first post.
6. You will also need to set up widgets along your sidebar. This prime advertising space (usually directly under the header) depending on the layout of the theme. Paste HTML code into text boxes of the widgets so that you can create adverts for the affiliate product or service that you're promoting. Your chosen merchant may even provide ready-made adverts that already have a hyperlink embedded into them.
7. Remember to use text hyperlinks inside your actual blog posts too so that prospects can click through to the seller's site. Hyperlink images to the products too.
8. List building – list building is essential for affiliate marketers. You want to effectively

build lists for future promotions. Include an opt in form on your blog (there are numerous free tools available on the Web). You can simply stick a text widget on your blog and paste the HTML code to the opt in form in it. Be sure to start building your list from the very first day.

2. Affiliate Landing Page

Many seasoned affiliate marketers will tell you that a unique and informational landing page is crucial in order to successfully promote affiliate products. A landing page is essentially a webpage that you set up to promote the product. When a prospect clicks on the advert, they are redirected to the tailored landing page instead of going straight through to the merchant's website.

A landing page typically displays content that is relevant to what the prospect is searching for, which means it is well optimized towards the specific content, product or service. A landing page allows you to offer more information relating to the product or service you're promoting – and you can use a variety of forms to do so. Reviews, as we've already mentioned, are extremely effective. So are videos. Whichever means you use, showing potential customers all the benefits that the product can offer in a personalized way encourages them to make a purchase. And when they're ready to make a purchase it's as easy as clicking on the affiliate link within your landing page.

3. Affiliate Marketing Website

Here is where you will be selling your affiliate marketing products from. If you've never run a website before, it's not daunting. In fact, all you need is hosting and a domain – just like the blog. Remember to avoid using copyright or trademarked words in your domain name. Typical domains cost around $10 per year. When you check out from choosing your domain, be sure to sign up for the domain privacy option which hides your personal information from the general public. Purchase hosting that will suit your needs for your website.

Once you have your domain and hosting your website will display a "coming soon" type of page. So you'll need to install a Content Management System (CMS) such as Joomla, Drupal or WordPress. CMS allows for super simple creation and updating of the website. Once you've installed a CMS you can upgrade it with themes to make it look like a top-notch website. Keep your site clean and simple when it comes to your layout, though. You want to make navigating the site as easy as possible for prospective buyers.

Different Types of Affiliate Marketing Websites

1. We can't emphasize enough how well product review websites work. It places you as an expert in the field and offers customers your personal opinions and insight on the products or services that you're promoting.
2. Everyone wants the best deal they can get their hands on, so product price comparisons sites also work well. This method can even be combined with product reviews.
3. Similar to product price comparisons are coupons and rebates. The method of offering coupons and rebates can be challenging though as some of the bigger name websites offer some seriously good incentives.
4. Affiliate marketers frequently use niche marketing sites. The sites are usually small to medium sized and focus on a very specific niche. It's usually something you would never have thought of which means it can work well as there is little to no competition.

Remember, you can choose one, or combine these types of websites for your affiliate product.

4. Killer Content Necessary!

You've surely heard the phrase "Content is King" and never is this more true than with affiliate marketing. Whether you're creating your website, blog, an e-book or building a mailing list, you're going to need refreshing, informative and enticing content. Content isn't just about copy though. Take a look at a few different types of content that you can utilize to promote your affiliate product or service:

- Videos

Why would you decide to use affiliate videos? Well, instead of just sending out emails or creating a copy-rich website with affiliate links, why not offer a video of testimonials or product demonstrations? Videos bring a degree of realism to the marketing and people are able to hear a voice and see faces. You bring credibility to the product or service. It's a fact that people prefer to purchase from people they recognize and trust and a video goes a long way to helping you build credibility with your visitors.

- Email Subject Lines

Email marketing can be massively effective, but only if you can get your list to open the email. So when it comes to emails, the subject line is possibly the most important piece of content.

- Pre-sells and Sales Letters

As an affiliate you wouldn't usually have to write full-blown sales copy for the product or service you're promoting. The merchant will do that. However, it's good to learn how to write compelling sales copy to incorporate into your article or blog posts.

- **Headlines**

You need killer headers that will grab attention and pull your visitors into wanting to know more about your affiliate product. If you're unsure about writing attention-grabbing copy, consider hiring a freelance writer from one of the many freelance websites out there.

Whatever type of content you're creating, you can be sure it is the key strategy that will help you to turn leads into buyers. In fact, content marketing has become the new affiliate marketing strategy and it is essential that you understand the importance of creating valuable content. Today, online buyers are not only looking for value but also trusted resources from which to make purchases. This is why content via videos, blogging and other elements just mentioned is so important.

Affiliate marketing is competitive and you need to gain a lot of traffic. Once you get that traffic they need to be convinced to make a purchase or sign up for a subscription or handover their contact details. So you need to offer them value – you need to focus on what really matters to your visitors. LOUD SALES COPY doesn't work anymore, nor does exaggeration. Shoppers are savvy. In fact, 80% of searchers know what they want and they know you have something to promote so they want a really good reason that will help sway them towards making a purchase through you.

It's been reported that the majority of those shoppers end up subscribing or purchasing due to the quality of content. Here are a few simple content marketing strategies:

a. Blogging

Blogging is a great platform for quality content. Best of all, it works!

b. Video

YouTube is effective, has a lot of traffic and shows no signs of slowing down.

c. Social Media

If worked properly, social media can really work! You don't even need thousands of likes, fans, followers or circles to be successful. Sharing quality content and really caring about your online communities is all that it takes to be effective.

Following these easy strategies for simple platforms can ensure that your content marketing can grow exponentially. Content marketing is not only a must for affiliate marketers but is the most powerful marketing strategy.

5. Google Analytics

Acquiring accurate analytics can be challenging for affiliates since the conversion usually happens on the merchant's site. So you cannot typically track conversions via Google Analytics.

There are some merchant programs that offer tracking systems but they're not as robust as analytics. The good news is that there are techniques that affiliate marketers can use with Google Analytics to capture valuable data and determine how to improve their content and ROI.

1. Tracking Email Signups

Typically, affiliate websites rely heavily on an email list or auto responder to capture visitor's contact details. Google Analytics is an effective tool for tracking email signups whenever you require visitors to provide an email address.

To set up email tracking you can set up a URL destination goal in your Google Analytics account that matches the thank you page visitors are presented with once they've signed up or opted-in.

2. Tracking Clicks on Affiliate Links

Although you may not be able to track affiliate sales with Google Analytics, you can certainly track when visitors click on your affiliate link to go through to the seller's website. With Analytics you can use a Javascript onclick event to track click-throughs.

To set this option up you can use virtual page views which tells Google Analytics to treat each time someone clicks on the link as if they are viewing a specified nonexistent webpage. An advantage of doing this is that you can track each click as a conversion if you wish to.

Alternatively, you can use events that allow you to track actions when a visitor clicks play on a video or when they click on a link. You can set up different event categories to track different links on your platform.

3. Tracking Clicks on Google Adsense Ads

Some affiliate marketers choose to monetize their sites through Adsense. You can link your Analytics and Adsense accounts so that you can see your Adsense stats in the analytics reports. This helps you to quickly see things like which pages, keywords and traffic sources are driving the most clicks and therefore the most profits.

4. Tracking Clicks on Other Adverts

If your blog or website displays ads other than Adsense, you're still able to track clicks. Use Google Analytics Events to track clicks in the same way you would for affiliate links.

Setting up Google Analytics can help you to analyze traffic sources and continue improving your ROI.

Setting Up Google Analytics on Your Website

1. Log in or sign up for a Google Account.
2. Once you've logged into your Google Account, head over to the Google analytics website and click the "Access Analytics" button. Click "sign up" to create an account for your website. You will then be asked to enter your account name, website URL and your time zone.
3. Google will ask if you want to share your data with other Google accounts such as AdWords and AdSense.
4. Next, set up the Tracking Code Configuration whereby you tell Analytics whether you're tracking a single domain or multiple domains with various other options.
5. Once the tracking code is configured you can install it onto your site. Depending on how the website is built, the installation procedure will vary. For example, if you run a WordPress website, some of the themes come complete with admin panels that allow you to easily copy the tracking code into the field designed for tracking scripts.

6. PayPal

Once you're up and running you will need an account into which your commission can be paid. A PayPal account is ideal as you can be paid in various currencies which are then converted into your home currency.

You only need two things to set up your PayPal account: an email address and a credit card.

1. Sign up – complete PayPal's sign up form and they will send you an email with a link for you to click on to confirm your email address.
2. You can then add your credit card details to your new account. PayPal stores the details for future transactions.

These are just 6 tools you need to get started as an affiliate marketer. Next we look at how to get those important leads.

4. Getting the Leads

The internet is a powerful business tool when it comes to growing your business with lead generation. But what is lead generation?

Online Lead Generation

Lead generation is a term used in internet marketing that describes the generation of customer interest into services or products.

The methods that are used in lead generation vary from tracking website visits to referrals and even search engine results. The quality of the lead is typically determined by the likelihood that it will generate a sale.

Lead generation can be used for other means too, such as building mailing lists and acquiring other information online for promoting your affiliate product or service. It is also used to increase traffic to websites, blogs and social media platforms.

When you start looking at lead generation for your affiliate marketing, you need to determine the type of lead that you want to work with. Marketing leads are normally retained through adverts and referrals.

Often, online leads can be purchased and are valued at price per thousand, price per action method or price per click. Such leads tend to take the form of banner ads or direct response advertisements.

Not all methods of lead generation are costly. There are a few free ways that you can acquire leads online. Most notably is through the organic or free results of the major search engines like Google, Yahoo and Bing. In order to achieve this, your site has to be properly optimized for the main keywords that are related to the affiliate product or service that you are promoting. Other free means of lead generation include videos; images; memes; social networks; forums and blogs. These means may cost nothing but they can do a great deal in turning a profit and raising awareness of your affiliate service or product.

Facebook Marketing

Facebook is a platform that has the ability to put you in touch with millions of individuals around the globe. It is therefore an extremely powerful marketing tool.

One of the biggest advantages of using Facebook for affiliate marketing is that you have the ability to gain a large amount of traffic in a fairly short period of time. Facebook advertising hasn't taken off in droves yet, which is perfect for you as the costs are still relatively low but the targeting ability is superb.

Facebook ads, according to founder Mark Zuckerberg, are a platform for affiliates and businesses to use targeted advertising. They offer the ability to connect precisely with the consumers you want.

There are two forms of Facebook ads:

1. **Paid advertising** – you can attach an ad message to user notifications. In order to direct your ad you can choose to target the traits that users have volunteered on their profiles such as interests, activities and age.
2. **User-initiated brand recommendations** – when people visit a page on Facebook, they announce their association to a brand by writing on the brand's wall or "liking" the page to become a fan. The philosophy here is that people are more likely to consider a brand that has been recommended by their friends and family.

So here's what Facebook can offer you as an affiliate marketer:

- *Simplicity* – it's quick and simple to create an ad in Facebook. All you do is write the copy for the ad and tell Facebook which market you want to reach and then decide where you want the traffic to be directed to (your blog, landing page or website, for example).

- *Reaching your target market* – the ads can be precisely targeted for your chosen audience.
- *Awareness* – Social Ads allow you the opportunity to become part of the daily conversation in people lives.
- *Content integration* – Facebook allows for your relevant content to appear on the surface.
- *Trusted referrals* – by associating your ads with friend-to-friend interaction, you can take advantage of the power of word-of-mouth.

A Few Facebook Marketing Tips

- You need to join Facebook before you start advertising on the platform. So you'll need to set up a personal profile before creating a business page. Begin by inviting friends and potential clients to be your friends.
- Set up your Business Page to begin targeted marketing. Enter your keywords carefully to ensure you attract your targeted demographic. Keyword optimization in Facebook also plays a role in search engine ranking.
- Make sure your adverts are specific and point to your website, blog or landing page.

- Join groups on Facebook that reflect your product or service, or even your prospect's interests.
- Strategically update your status a few times a day to show you are an active Facebook user. This also helps to push information out into your follower's feeds. This works well if you link your profile to your website. Whenever you update your website, blog or landing page, or want to promote your affiliate product, post it as a status update.
- Comment on your community's links, videos and photos to ignite conversations.
- Add value to your followers by positioning yourself as an expert with regards to the affiliate product or service you are marketing. Post relevant links and information.

Solo Ads

You may have heard of solo ads but aren't too sure what they are or how you can use them for affiliate marketing.

Solo ads are ads that stand alone in the form of advertorials. They are published in reputable ezines that typically have a significant following. Your ad is the only advertising on the specific page so it is more likely that it will be viewed. Factors to consider when thinking about solo ads for your marketing include: frequency of publication; number of subscribers and general interest of the readers. For example, you won't want to advertise a breakthrough pet product in an automobile ezine!

Solo ads are relatively inexpensive (the costs can run from free to $3 per thousand impressions) and targeted placement is a major benefit as you are able to target your solo ad specifically to your market. In essence, those people have opted in to receive the ezine and expect to see offers like yours, so there is less chance of your ad being considered spam. Solo ads are a good way to reach lots of people for very little outlay of cash.

If you want to look into solo ads for your affiliate marketing, make sure you have a precise plan as opposed to putting out generic, hyped up offerings. Deliver quality and promise a lot more information for those who wish to know more – and be sure to follow up on that. Create a tracking system so you can determine which ads are successful and which aren't along with which ezines are proving effective and which are not.

Solo ads are a fantastic way to drive visitors to your offers.

Pay-Per-Click Marketing

Pay-per-click (PPC) marketing is highly competitive for affiliates. Since online marketing is a great deal about ranking tops amongst the search engines, a good keyword management solution can help you with the ability to segment and manage literally millions of keywords in just minutes. Powerful keyword grouping and organization tools will help you to improve your results and keyword efficiency.

In order to make a living as an affiliate marketer, you need to continuously practice keyword searches to ensure that you are using the right keywords for your platforms. There are a number of tools on the internet that will help you to analyze keyword searches and to determine their profitability. Choose a keyword management tool that will view search engine optimization and PPC efforts as complementary.

Your PPC affiliate marketing efforts can be applied towards your standard SEO (Search Engine Optimization) too. Track your best performing PPC keywords and use them for on-page SEO.

5. How to Find an Affiliate Program That's Right for You

Affiliate marketing may be competitive but it retains a lucrative appeal. With literally hundreds of thousands of affiliate programs out there, how do you, as an affiliate, choose the best one or ones to join?

Firstly, let's look at the major items to consider when looking for a potentially profitable affiliate program to join:

1. The Product or Service

Most importantly, pick a product that interests you. Something you're not interested in is bound to have you giving up quickly if things don't initially work. You need to feel passionate, even if it's a little, about the product or service you want to promote since you are going to spend a substantial amount of time talking about it and promoting it.

As important as your interest level in the product or service is other people's interest. Is it something that is in demand? Make use of Google's keyword tool to determine which keywords are being searched for along with the estimated search volume each word receives monthly. You can also analyze the level of competition for your specific keywords.

If the competition is high but the search volume is fairly low, considering passing on that particular product or service. But if the search volume is consistently high and the competition relatively low, it might be just the ticket to your financial freedom.

2. Website

Once you've decided on the affiliate program you'd like to join and that there is sufficient demand for the service or product in the marketplace, take a look at the merchant's website.

Consider elements such as its user-friendliness and ease to navigate. Does the website consist of clear messages? Are there calls to action? Are images and products clearly displayed so that consumers know what they are buying?

Also, take note as to whether or not the website has any leaks. Leaks are actually paths or links that take a visitor out of the website – they won't generate any money for you. Links could lead to other non-commissionable websites as opposed to leading to a checkout or confirmation page. These are areas where you could potentially lose money and sales.

If you are going to be representing someone's website, make sure it is reputable and has potential for a strong sales-based performance for you.

3. Conversion Rate

Conversion rates are arguably one of the most important numbers to look at when choosing an affiliate program. The merchant that you are considering may have a fantastic website, a solid brand and an extremely enticing commission offer, but, if the website does not convert, then you aren't going to make money promoting it.

Conversion is calculated by the amount of people who complete a call to action out of 100. For example, if one person out of 100 completes an order on the website, the conversion rate is just 1%. This is pretty much the average for eCommerce sites but it's not necessarily a good thing. Do keep in mind the cost of the product and the commission you are going to earn. As an affiliate, the ideal is a conversion rate of more than 3% in order turn a healthy profit.

4. Commission or Payout

This is the number that draws the most attention. Too often affiliates will join programs that have high commission payouts and overlook the lower ones. But this doesn't necessarily work in your favor. Do your homework and math and find which affiliate program is going to really turn your desired profit.

5. Average Order Value

This is where you can earn the most money.

If, for example, Merchant A pays out 10% commission with an average 1% conversion rate but Merchant B pays out 12% commission and has an average 3% conversion rate, most people will rush to join Merchant B. But, Merchant A's Average Order Value is actually $380 whereas Merchant A's is only $100.

So Merchant A's product will pay out $12 per sale, whereas Merchant B's payout will be just $36. It goes without saying that Merchant A will be the one to join.

Look closely at Average Order Values before determining which affiliate program you want to join.

6. Earnings Per Click (EPC)

It is important to ask the merchant what their EPC is. EPC will show the average earning potential from the affiliate program based on affiliates who are already a part of the program.

You can calculate EPC by dividing the overall commission that is generated by the number of clicks.

So let's say that you receive a commission of $15 after sending 100 clicks to the merchant's site. Divide that $15 by 100 and you get 0.15. Your EPC is therefore $0.15 per click.

This figure depicts exactly how much you will earn for each visitor you send to the merchant. So it is essential that you work it out before deciding which program to join.

7. Duration of Cookies

The length of the affiliate cookies is another important element to consider. Cookies are a tracking method that is used by the merchant and is hidden on the merchant's website. The purpose of the cookies is to track the customers that were referred by you to the merchant's website through your affiliate link or code so that you can be credited with the sale or the click and paid a commission when a either a product that you are promoting is purchased or someone clicks on your affiliate link to reach the merchant's website.

If the seller offers a 30 day cookie, the customer has 30 days to return to the seller in order to complete their purchase if they did not complete the purchase during the first visit to the website. Then you are still eligible for commission for that order. However, if a customer returns to the seller's website once the cookie has expired, you do not get commission for that sale. So, the longer the cookie is the better.

8. Tools

Try to find a merchant that offers a decent variety of high quality tools that you can use. Such tools include text links; banners; coupons; search boxes; videos; data feeds and widgets. In other words, make sure the seller offers valuable tools that help you to do your job. If you don't have good tools to market with it is much more difficult to drive traffic from your platform to the seller's website.

9. Reversal Rates

Reversal rates tell you the percentage of orders that were returned, cancelled or un-commissioned. This is an important number. If a merchant has a 70% reversal rate, it means that 70% of orders that affiliates sent them were not credited for whatever reason.

Beware of high reversal rates. Your work will go unpaid and your time and investment will go down the drain. A slow conversion rate is normal for many programs and sure, sometimes orders are cancelled or returned – it's all part of the buying process that you need to be aware of.

Should you suddenly experience a high reversal rate when there wasn't one previously, ask your affiliate manager why the rate is suddenly so high. If they can't offer you a good reason, or you feel something isn't quite right with the explanation, consider changing affiliate programs.

10. Competition

Consider how competitive the marketplace is for the product or service you're considering marketing. Also, keep an eye on what the competition is doing. Often there are multiple merchant's offering the same product and services and they all trying to recruit top affiliates. Seek out and choose the ones that offer higher payouts and have better conversions.

Also keep in mind that if a product has a great deal of affiliates promoting it, it's going to be challenging for you to capture a big market share in terms of sales since many other affiliates will be promoting the same product and competing for the same traffic..

11. Terms of Service

Don't overlook the terms of service in order to quickly agree to having read it. Every program has different terms which outline how you can market the affiliate links, how those links can be placed, keywords you can and cannot use and whether you can link to the merchant's website using a direct search or if you can indeed promote their program at all via search. The terms of service will also outline the software you can and can't use.

12. Support

Another important thing to note when selecting an affiliate program is whether or not they offer a dedicated affiliate manager. It is ideal to have a knowledgeable affiliate manager in charge of the program but it's even better to have a knowledgeable affiliate manager who is there when you need them to answer your questions.

Look for things in an affiliate manager such as their ability to be reached via telephone or via email or IM. Consider their response times and their experience and understanding of how this type of marketing works. Find out if they have a keen understanding of the terms of service and their ability to guide you when you have questions and concerns. Also consider their ability to get you the tools you need in a timely fashion so that you can effectively begin marketing and making money.

The best way to do this is call or email the manager and see how quickly they respond, if at all.

6. Popular Affiliate Programs

As we've established, affiliate marketing is a relatively easy way to make money online. Since you, as an affiliate, are not required to offer your own product or service, you are free from many of the responsibilities and complications of the more traditional sales models. Below are 10 of the most popular affiliate programs.

1. Clickbank

Clickbank boasts more than 100 000 affiliates selling products from over 10 000 vendors. So there is a great deal of money being made by both the merchants and affiliates. The vendors are raking in cash because they have troops of affiliates marketing and selling their products. The affiliates are enjoying lucrative income from simply selling an already existing product. This product comes in a digital format so it can be delivered online via web pages, email or files.

Besides promoting the vendor's products, Clickbank affiliates can make money by promoting and referring new customers via the Clickbank reseller program.

You can promote a Clickbank product by using a "hoplink." This hoplink consists of a mixture of your Clickbank username and the vendor's name. When the customer clicks on the hoplink, they are directed to the vendor's sales page. When they make a purchase, your commission is tracked automatically.

You can insert the hoplink on your website or in the place where you are promoting the product. For example: if you're promoting a product that removes computer viruses, you can write an article about the different types of computer viruses that exists and can infect a computer and at the end of that article you can recommend a product that removes those particular viruses. All you would have to do is include your hoplink and they will be directed towards the merchant's website. If a purchase is made you get a commission.

You can also insert your promotion that includes the hoplink as a footer in your email communication.

2. Linkshare

This affiliate program launched in 1996 and is today one of the largest affiliate networks on the World Wide Web. Once you join the network you are given access to a huge variety of merchants and products. You can then select items and place links on your website. Every time someone clicks one of those links and makes a purchase you earn a commission on the total amount of the sale.

3. Amazon Associates

Amazon.com's affiliate program is known as Associates. Amazon associates (aka affiliates) drive traffic to Amazon.com via specially formatted links that allow Amazon to track sales. Associates are paid up to 10% referral fees on qualifying revenue that is generated by their affiliate links.

4. Commission Junction

This is the supermarket of the affiliate world! You need a website to be able to join Commission Junction and get the best out of the program. You can sign up for free and then opt into the different affiliate programs. As a website owner, you can make commission in a number of ways depending on the program you decide to join.

- You can earn money for every click-through on an affiliate banner running on your site.
- You can earn money for every search made from your site using an affiliate search box.
- You can be paid a set fee for every sale made as a result of an affiliate ad running on your website.

You can join as many affiliate programs as you like on Commission Junction.

5. RevenueWire

This is an affiliate network that specializes in digital products. Their belief is that digital merchandise is easier to sell and purchase and they carry some of the most current and best-known brands in the digital world.

6. **Ebay Partner Network**

Becoming an Ebay Partner Network affiliate means you can earn money by driving high quality traffic to Ebay or anyone of their partners.

7. **ShareASale**

This is an affiliate marketing network that is based in Chicago, Illinois. ShareASale provides pay-per-lead; pay-per-sale and PPC programs for webmasters.

8. **OneNetworkDirect**

OneNetworkDirect from Digital River is the leader in software sales with the industry's best network technology and offices worldwide.

9. **AvantLink**

AvantLink is another popular affiliate network that really looks after their affiliates.

10. **Google Affiliate Network**

This is a free program that makes it easy for affiliates to connect with reputable advertisers and be rewarded for driving conversions. Google's name and credibility alone lends to many people seeing the advantage of affiliating with Google's network. You need to have an AdSense account to be able to join the network and Google will review your website to determine if it meets the standards and can fulfill the requirements for partnership.

One more affiliate program that is soaring in popularity and is worth a mention is Empower Network.

Although a relatively new program, Empower Network offers affiliates 100% of every sale. They operate on referral and blogging systems. The blogging system is based around the idea that you create quality content and post that content to your blog and then share it to drive visitors to the blog.

Your blog is set up instantly when you join the network and it's already optimized. The blog comes with training videos that promise to fast track your learning and progress and help you to get started with the network. The initial outlay required to join the network is relatively low.

There are literally thousands of affiliate programs out there. Remember to do your research to find the one or ones that best suit you.

7. Mistakes New Affiliate Marketers Should Avoid

If done right, affiliate marketing can be very profitable. But there are a number of mistakes than can ruin your chances for success. Below are just some of those mistakes that you can avoid.

1. Thinking You're Going to Get Rich Quickly

Affiliate marketing is certainly not a golden ticket to limitless, endless and effortless wealth. In fact, affiliate marketing takes work to promote your marketing platforms (website, landing page, social networks, blog) and to get traffic as well as generating click-throughs. If you want to make loads of cash with minimal work, then this type of marketing is not going to be for you.

2. Assuming People Will Just Visit Your Site

There are millions of websites on the internet. Sitting and waiting for traffic is going to prove fruitless. You need to be proactive and make use of techniques such as social media marketing, SEO and link building in order to get your site noticed and ranked and get people clicking on the affiliate links.

3. Bombarding Your Audience

If you're showing your audience more advertisement than content, then you can rest assured they won't be coming back any time soon. Too many banners can also make a page appear confusing and unorganized. This is why you should only pick a handful of reputable affiliate partners within your niche and stick with them to avoid clutter.

4. On the Other Hand: Not Providing Enough Material

Just as you shouldn't bombard your audience with advertisements that can annoy and confuse them, not offering enough interesting, fresh and informational material can have the adverse effect on your marketing efforts. Less is definitely more but don't make your page so empty that it's boring or you'll see your traffic dwindling rapidly and your affiliate income becoming virtually non-existent.

5. Not Measuring Performance

You cannot know if your marketing efforts are working properly unless you regularly monitor your results. It is critical that you analyze your individual campaigns to determine whether or not you are on the right track or if you need to make any adjustments to your marketing strategy.

6. Neglecting To Gauge Your Competition

Although affiliate marketing isn't a cut-throat business, per se, there are other affiliates out there that are trying to do the same thing as you. Learn from them. See what mistakes they make and what seems to work for them. A little bit of healthy competition is bound to do wonders for your bottom line.

7. Not Choosing Your Affiliate Partners Carefully

You don't want to ruin your reputation and credibility with the audience that you have acquired through your marketing or promotion by referring them to a merchant that is unscrupulous and has a bad reputation. This can negatively impact on your audience so be careful who you partner with.

8. Not Providing Your Audience with Quality Content

Getting traffic to your marketing platforms is only half the battle. Keeping them coming back is what counts. Many affiliate marketers make the mistake of populating their sites with stagnant, irrelevant and outdated content. If readers don't feel that they are getting value out of the content that you're providing, chances are they won't be back and they are even less likely to refer anyone else to your site.

9. Not Understanding What You're Promoting

The bottom line is you have to understand what you are promoting and its benefits, because if you don't understand what you are promoting, how can you expect the people you are trying to influence to have the confidence that is necessary to part with their dollars?

10. Overselling to Your Market

Sure, the whole point of affiliate marketing is to make money. But people abhor a pushy salesperson. You don't want your visitors to lose interest because your posts are too sales pitchy. Instead, your aims should be to offer assistance and advice. Build a rapport with your audience as opposed to pushing them towards a sale.

The word 'marketing' may be part of the phrase *affiliate marketing* but your job is not to sell. As an affiliate it is your job to drive leads to the merchant's site.

11. Making False Claims

You've probably seen it before: a person on a forum about online marketing posts a complaint about not being able to make money online. But scroll down and their signature line will entail something about them making millions of dollars with a certain program followed by the affiliate link.

Don't be that person that makes false claims. If you're new to the world of affiliate marketing and want to promote products in the online arena, avoid such claims! By all means discuss the benefits of the product or service; even mention why it sounds so good to you. But do not trick people. You will only serve to ruin your credibility.

If you put in the work and effort, affiliate marketing can be an extremely lucrative way to make money online. It's not fool-proof though. Nor is it straightforward. By being aware of these common mistakes novices make, you will be less likely to follow those who have failed and far more likely to be a success story.

Becoming an Affiliate Marketer

You may not know much about the internet and you may know very little about making money online but with affiliate marketing you can discover a world that can become not only your new business but a passion too.

Now that you know what affiliate marketing is, how to become an affiliate marketer and the mistakes to avoid, it's time to choose the programs that interest you. It really is as simple as signing up with a merchant and getting to work promoting the products or services in order to enjoy a substantial monthly income. In fact, you can make a full time income just from affiliate marketing!

As an affiliate marketer you can enjoy working from anywhere in the world as long as you have an internet connection and it costs virtually nothing to get started

There are affiliates out there making monthly incomes in the region of $10 000 – $50 000 and this is common amongst the advanced marketers.

If you want to become a successful affiliate marketer, be prepared to put in the work. Ensure that this type of marketing is something you want to do – do your homework and learn all you can about the different aspects of affiliate marketing.

Most importantly, stay focused and if you prudently and wisely invest in your affiliate business it will grow along with your revenue.

Other Books Available By Author On Kindle, Audio and Paperback

The Killer Instinct: How To Master It and Achieve Anything That You Want

Conquering Your Fears

Money Magnet: How To Use The Laws Of The Universe To Attract Money Into Your Life

How To Create A Profitable Ezine From Scratch

The Secrets Of Making $10,000 on Ebay in 30 Days

The Complete Guide To Investing in Gold And Silver: Surviving The Great Economic Depression

How To Sell Any Product Online:"Secrets of The Killer Sales Letter"

How To Make A Fortune Using The Public Domain

Search Engine Domination: The Ultimate Secrets To Increasing Your Website's Visibility And Making A Ton Of Cash

Creative Real Estate Investing Strategies And Tips

How to Make Money Online:"The Savvy Entrepreneur's Guide To Financial Freedom"

How to Overcome Your Self-Limiting Beliefs & Achieve Anything You Want

The Secrets of Finding The Perfect Ghostwriter For Your Book

The Creative Real Estate Marketing Equation: Motivated Sellers + Motivated Buyers = $

How To Start An Online Business With Less Than $200

How To Market Your Business Online and Offline

Money Blueprint: The Secrets To Creating Instant Wealth

How To Promote Market And Sell Your Kindle Book

AudioBook Profits: How To Make Money by Turning Your Kindle, Paperback and Hardcover Book into Audio.

The Fine Art of Writing The Next Best Seller on Kindle

Fast Cash: 9 Amazing Ways To Make Money Without Having To Work At A Job